PANZERS IN THE DESERT

An early PzKpfw IIIJ with short-barrelled 5 cm KwK L/42 gun. The 15th Panzer Division insignia can just be seen next to the crewman's right foot (438/1189/7).

BRUCE QUARRIE
PANZERS IN THE DESERT

WORLD
WAR
2
PHOTO
ALBUM
NUMBER 1

A selection of German wartime photographs
from the Bundesarchiv, Koblenz

PSL Patrick Stephens, Cambridge

First published in 1978

British Library Cataloguing in Publication Data
Panzers in the desert. – (World War 2
    photo albums; 1).
    1. Germany. Heer. Afrikakorps – Pictorial
    works   2. World War, 1939–45 – Campaigns
    – Africa, North – Pictorial works
    I. Quarrie, Bruce   II. Series
    940.54'23   D766.82

    ISBN 0 85059 338 7 (casebound)
    ISBN 0 85059 315 8 (softbound)

Design by Tim McPhee

Photoset in 10pt Plantin Roman. Printed in Great
Britain on 100gsm Pedigree coated cartridge and
bound by The Garden City Press Limited,
Letchworth, Hertfordshire, SG6 1JS, for the
publishers, Patrick Stephens Limited, Bar Hill,
Cambridge, CB3 8EL.

CONTENTS

Acknowledgements
The author and publisher would like to express their sincere thanks to Dr Matthias Haupt and Herr Meinrad Nilges of the Bundesarchiv for their assistance, without which this book would have been impossible.

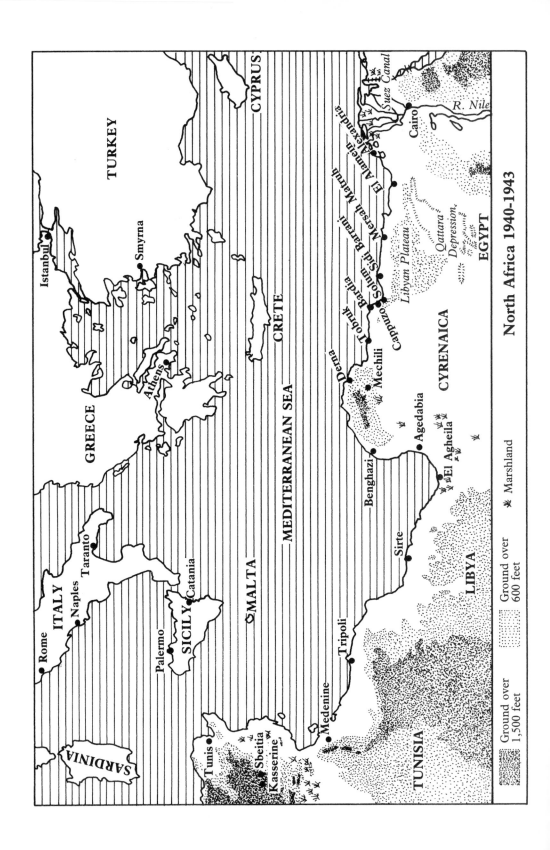

North Africa 1940-1943

Few men are granted the privilege of becoming legends within their own lifetimes, but Erwin Rommel was one. A successful and much-decorated infantry officer in World War 1, he came to the early notice of Adolf Hitler and rose to the command of a Panzer division during the German invasion of France in 1940. His natural grasp of the tactics required in modern armoured warfare made him a logical choice as commander of the German expeditionary force sent to Africa in 1941, and within months he had become as highly respected among his English and Commonwealth adversaries as he was among his own troops.

Following the severe trouncing which Italian troops in the desert had experienced at the hands of Wavell's forces during the closing months of 1940, Hitler decided in January 1941 to send a German 'blocking force' to North Africa, and Rommel was selected as its commander. The immediate and dramatic reversal of situations which occurred once the Germans arrived in the theatre can be attributed to four main factors: Rommel's own drive and inspired leadership; superior German morale in comparison with their Italian allies; the severely over-extended British lines of communication; and the fact that Wavell's forces had been denuded of many veteran units because of the situation in the Balkans.

It is unnecessary here to go into the see-saw details of the North African campaign because they have been so endlessly repeated in numerous other publications. Suffice to say that the Germans drove the over-extended Allies back into Egypt but failed to take the important port of Tobruk, and were then themselves pushed back to Mersa Brega at the end of 1941. They counter-attacked at the beginning of 1942, forcing the Allies back to the Gazala line; a series of confused armoured battles occupied most of the summer of 1942, resulting in an eventual Allied withdrawal and German pursuit to the Alamein position at the end of June, by which time Tobruk had also fallen to the Axis. The first, inconclusive, battle of Alamein was fought during July; Montgomery was then appointed in command of the 8th Army under Alexander and spent two months regrouping and building up his forces. He launched the second battle of Alamein in October and had the Axis in rout by early November, shortly after which Anglo-American forces landed by sea in Morocco. The Germans and Italians then retreated steadily, were reinforced by new units, and fought a stubborn campaign in Tunisia, but were finally forced to capitulate in May 1943.

Throughout this period, the nucleus of the Axis forces were the 15th and 21st Panzer Divisions which, together with 90th Light Division, formed the 'Deutsches Afrika-Korps' (DAK); other German and Italian units present fell under command of Panzergruppe Afrika, later renamed Panzerarmee Afrika, 1st Italienische Armee and finally Heeresgruppe Afrika. Although titular control fluctuated, and the DAK – which retained its individual identity within the higher formations – had its own commanders (Crüwell, Nehring, Bayerlein, von Vaerst, von Thoma, etc), effective control was in Rommel's own hands throughout most of the campaign.

The vast open wastes of the North African desert form an almost ideal battleground, comprising wide spaces for tactical manoeuvre with no crowded urban areas to interfere with the serious business of fighting. Being largely flat they are also excellent for fast-moving armoured battles, although sand, dust and heat take their toll of both men and machines. Thanks to these factors, plus the inherent decency of commanders on both sides, the war in the desert was, insofar as the business of killing ever can be, a chivalrous and gentlemanly conflict. Both sides had immense respect for each other, prisoners and wounded were well-treated, and there were no major atrocities; the abrasive, cleansing effect of 'the blue' enforced a code of conduct unseen in any other theatre of the war.

Hence the seemingly endless fascination among modern military historians and enthusiasts on both sides of the Atlantic, and hence this book, in which I have tried to show the campaign through German eyes using the extensive photographic resources of the Bundesarchiv – about which more in a moment. The title of the book is 'Panzers in the desert' so there are a few pictures of Italian and British tanks, but the emphasis is on German vehicles and personnel.

The most widely used German tank in North Africa was the PzKpfw III (SdKfz 141), the first production model of which had been completed in 1936 (Ausf A). After various development modifications the first major production version (Ausf F) appeared in early 1940, fitted with a 3·7 cm gun. Later in the same year the Ausf G, equipped with a short-barrelled 5 cm gun (L/42), entered production, and it was this version which accompanied the first German tank formations in the desert. The basic PzKpfw III weighed just under 20 tons and carried a crew of five (driver, radio operator, gunner, loader and commander); powered by a 12-cylinder Maybach engine producing 300 bhp at 3,000 rpm through a ten-speed gearbox, it was capable of attaining 40 km/h with an average fuel consumption of 187 litres per 100 kilometres giving a range of up to 165 kilometres depending on the ground (although evaporation and other factors reduced this to around 95 kilometres in the desert). Its armour plate varied from 16 mm on its hull bottom to 30 mm on hull and turret vertical surfaces (maximum 25 degree slope on turret sides). In addition to its 5 cm L/42 main gun the tank mounted a bow and a turret co-axial MG 34 machine-gun of 7·92 mm calibre. Those machines sent to North Africa were equipped with additional air filters and a different coolant fan reduction ratio.

Most of the PzKpfw IIIs sent to this theatre in the early stages, however, were Ausf H or J versions with wider tracks, new sprockets and idlers, re-spaced return rollers and additional 30 mm armour plates on hull and turret front faces. Later production Ausf Js were also fitted with the longer-barrelled 5 cm KwK 39 L/60 main weapon, as were the Ausf L and M variants. Ammunition stowage varied from 99 to 78 rounds depending on type as the up-gunning and other modifications reduced the internal stowage space. Versions armed with the L/60 weapon were christened 'Mark III Specials' by the British because of the significantly increased penetration power of the long-barrelled weapon – 61 mm at 500 yards' range compared with 56 mm. This was mainly due to an increase in muzzle velocity from 685 to 823

metres per second and only partly to the slightly heavier shell fired by the L/60.

Ausf J–L models were heavier than earlier PzKpfw IIIs due to the larger gun and additional spaced armour plate (22·3 tons), and featured six instead of ten forward gears; other differences, such as the deletion of vision slits and lower hull escape hatches on the Ausf M (which appeared in 1942) made little if any difference to the vehicle's performance and capabilities. The basic PzKpfw III was a well-constructed design but nowhere near as superior to British tanks in the desert as has sometimes been made out. Its armour was comparable to that of the Crusader, thinner than that of the Matilda; its speed was superior to the latter, inferior to the former; and at normal desert battlefield ranges, the short-barrelled 5 cm gun was really no better than the British 2 pdr, except for the fact that it was capable of firing high explosive as well as armour-piercing ammunition – a capability lacked by British tanks until the introduction of the American 75 mm M1 and M2 weapons in the Lee/Grant and Sherman.

Variants on the basic PzKpfw III tank chassis included the StuG III assault gun, of which a few saw service in North Africa (reports vary from a mere three to six-plus, but at the outside it was only a couple of troops). The StuGs, like most self-propelled guns of World War 2, were designed to preserve the life of semi-obsolescent tank chassis by equipping them with heavier weapons in fixed armoured superstructures with limited traverse. Those StuG IIIs in Africa seem to have been early variants armed with short-barrelled 7·5 cm infantry support guns. Some PzKpfw III command vehicles (conversions from pre-production Ausf Ds) were also used in the desert; these had dummy main armament and extra radio equipment.

Supporting the PzKpfw IIIs in North Africa were smaller numbers of PzKpfw IIs and IVs. The former was a light reconnaissance vehicle which had first appeared in 1935 armed with a 20 mm main gun and designated SdKfz 121. Based on an MAN design, it was a seven-ton vehicle carrying a crew of three; its six-cylinder Maybach engine produced 130 bhp at 2,600 rpm, driving it at up to 40 km/h via a six-speed gearbox. Later models had more powerful engines (140 bhp) and weighed just under eight tons (Ausf B) while others (Ausf D/E) had torsion bar suspension and a top speed of

55 km/h. The Ausf F, with armour plate increased from 14·5 to between 20 and 35 mm, appeared at the end of 1940 and weighed 9·5 tons. As with the PzKpfw III, various types of suspension and numbers of road wheels were tried, the most successful being that used on the Ausf F, G and J with five independently sprung bogies each side: these were the tanks most commonly used in Africa.

While the PzKpfw II was a robust and useful vehicle in the reconnaissance role, its 20 mm armament would not allow it to put up much of a fight in any direct tank-versus-tank encounter. However, some of the Ausf Ds and Es which had been modified to flamethrowers in 1940 were later further converted into self-propelled guns by fitting modified Russian 76·2 mm weapons in lightly armoured open-topped fighting compartments, as was also done with the Czech PzKpfw 38(t) tank (Marder II and III). Later versions of these improvised vehicles also mounted German 7·5 cm Pak 40 anti-tank guns, but these were chiefly used in Russia. PzKpfw IIs were also modified to carry 10·5 cm howitzers under the designation 'Wespe' (Wasp).

Of all German tanks produced during World War 2, the most significant was unquestionably the PzKpfw IV (SdKfz 161); not because it was the best, but simply because it was the most versatile and manufactured in larger quantities through successive modifications than any other design. The PzKpfw IV arose as the result of a design proposal in 1934 for a support tank mounting a gun larger than the 3·7 cm weapon envisaged for the PzKpfw III. As in the case of the PzKpfw II and III, various firms submitted design proposals, and Krupp (who had lost the PzKpfw III contract to Daimler-Benz and the PzKpfw II to MAN) finally prevailed. It is a tribute to the soundness of the original design that the basic suspension (paired bogies on longitudinal elliptical springs, with four return rollers) remained unaltered throughout the war. The tank was externally very similar in appearance to the PzKpfw III and only slightly larger, while internally it was driven by the same 12-cylinder Maybach engine through a five-speed gearbox giving a top speed of 30 km/h. The crew was five, as in the PzKpfw III, but the PzKpfw IV's main armament was a short-barrelled 7·5 cm gun for which 122 rounds of ammunition were carried. Armour

thickness on the first production version varied from 14·5 to 20 mm which was grossly inadequate; it was raised to 30 mm frontal on the Ausf B onwards, and a more powerful engine with six-speed gearbox fitted to cope with the extra weight.

The experience of the Polish campaign showed that this armour was still insufficient so the Ausf E was up-armoured to 60 mm frontal and 30–40 mm on the sides, increasing the vehicle's all-up weight to 22 tons. On the Ausf F the frontal armour reached 80 mm (50 mm plus 30 mm appliqué), and other changes included wider tracks, new welded-tubing sprockets and different-pattern idlers. The turret was also modified so as to be able to accommodate the long-barrelled 7·5 cm tank gun KwK 40 L/43 in place of the L/24. Ausf F vehicles with the latter weapon were designated F1 and those with the former F2; both saw extensive service in the desert. The muzzle velocity of the L/43 weapon was more than double that of the L/24, 990 metres per second compared with 450; the range was 8,100 compared with 6,500 metres (HE, not AP); and armour-piercing capability was 89 mm at 500 yards' range compared with only 41 mm for the L/24. The only visible difference between the Ausf F2 and the Ausf G, which was the last production version of the PzKpfw IV to see action in North Africa, was its double baffle muzzle brake. Later variants of the PzKpfw IV, from March 1943 onwards, were fitted with apron armour and the longer L/48 7·5 cm gun. Self-propelled guns on the PzKpfw IV chassis, such as the StuG IV, Jagdpanzer IV and various anti-aircraft vehicles, did not enter production until after the demise of the Afrika Korps.

Apart from the little machine-gun armed PzKpfw I, which saw limited service in Africa as a reconnaissance and command vehicle, the only other tank of significance in the theatre was the Tiger I (SdKfz 181) which equipped the 501st Independent Heavy Tank Battalion in Tunisia. (A few PzKpfw Is fitted with Czech 4·7 cm anti-tank guns as SPs also saw service in the desert.) The Tiger I had been designed by Henschel as the result of a specification issued by Hitler in May 1941 for a heavily armoured 45-ton tank mounting a version of the highly effective 8·8 cm anti-aircraft gun, and the prototype was put through its paces at Rastenburg on the Führer's birthday in April the following year.

When production began in August 1942, the Tiger I was unquestionably the most powerful tank in the world. Those which saw action in Tunisia were driven by a 21-litre, 12-cylinder Maybach engine which was not, in fact, man enough for the task, and later Tigers (December 1943 onwards) had a 24-litre engine. The Tiger had a pre-selector gearbox with eight forward gears which made it comparatively easy to handle despite its size and weight (55 tons). Those in North Africa were specially fitted with Feifel engine air cleaners.

The vehicle had a complicated system of interleaved and overlapping road wheels on independently sprung torsion bars which gave a very smooth ride, although its top speed was only 28 km/h. It carried a crew of five, had armour plate ranging from 26 mm (roof and floor) to 110 mm (mantlet). (Frontal armour was 100 mm, sides and rear 60 to 82 mm.) The tank carried 92 rounds of ammunition for its 8·8 cm KwK 36 L/56 main armament. This remarkable weapon fired a 9·4 kg shell, had a muzzle velocity of 810 metres per second and could penetrate 110 mm of armour plate at 500 yards' range.

The first tanks to arrive in North Africa were painted in the standard Wehrmacht dark grey colour, but in the following month were ordered to be over-painted in a sandy-brown shade. Grey-green was also available for disruptive camouflage over-painting, but does not appear to have been widely used. The usual German national crosses in black, black and white or plain white appeared on tank hull sides, and turret numbers in red or black and white. Divisional markings normally appeared on hull front and rear, sometimes also on the turrets, and practically every vehicle carried one or another of the numerous versions of the Afrika Korps' unique palm tree and swastika emblem. Tactical markings were widely applied to all vehicles except tanks, on which their use was rare. Wheeled and semi-tracked vehicles had standard Wehrmacht or Luftwaffe number plates. Aerial recognition flags – red, with a black swastika in a white circle – were widely used during those periods when the Luftwaffe was strong, less commonly as the Allied Desert Air Force acquired aerial supremacy.

There is insufficient space here to go into the subject of Italian AFVs in the desert, although they were also widely used by the Germans. These included the tiny CV L3 tankette, the M11/39, M13/40 and M14/41 medium tanks and the excellent Semovente M40/41/42 series of self-propelled guns. Poor quality armour plate, chronic mechanical unreliability and inadequate armament characterised most Italian armoured fighting vehicles, and it is a tribute to the courage of their oft-maligned crews that they were actually taken into battle.

A few miscellaneous AFVs, such as the Lorraine Schlepper in particular (a 15 cm gun mounted on a captured French chassis), also saw widespread service in North Africa.

When one comes to consider the detailed organisation of German armoured forces in the desert one runs into enormous problems, not only because *ad hoc* formations were created and disbanded practically daily for particular tasks, but also because the atrocious supply situation, high rate of mechanical breakdown and battle attrition left most units with little actual resemblance to their theoretical Order of Battle. For example, a Panzer regiment was supposed to have a complement of two battalions, each of two light and one medium companies, with around 20 tanks to a company, but in November 1941, for example, after the battle of Sidi Rezegh, 15th and 21st Panzer Divisions could not muster more than 100 tanks of all types between them; while when Rommel arrived at El Alamein in July 1942 they could only scrape together 58 serviceable vehicles! Contrast this with the fact that 5th Panzer Regiment had 150 tanks on strength when it arrived in Tripoli and you see the extent of the problem. Basically, however, the companies were organised into troops, each of five tanks plus a company headquarters section. The turret numbering system reflects this organisation perfectly: '123', for example, would be the No 3 tank in the 2nd Troop of the 1st Company. The zero numeral was used for HQ tanks, eg, R01 = regimental commander, R02 = regimental adjutant, I01 = 1st Battalion commander, II02 = 2nd Battalion adjutant, etc.

German tactical doctrine, and Rommel's concept of armoured warfare in particular, demanded very close co-operation between tanks and anti-tank guns, the latter being used offensively right up in the front line rather than defensively to the flanks and rear, as was British practice. German anti-tank guns were superior to anything the British could muster until the advent of the 17 pdr, not only in armour-piercing capability but also in their ability to fire high explosive. Admittedly, the little 3·7 cm Pak 35/36 L/45 was not very effective, and the frontal armour of the British Matilda defeated everything except the superb 7·5 cm Pak 40 or the 8·8 cm Flak 18/36, but the 5 cm Pak 38 L/42 and later L/60 were both excellent medium anti-tank guns which could penetrate 56 or 86 mm of armour plate respectively at 500 yards' range. The Pak 35/36, in comparison, could only penetrate 43 mm at the same range. However, the 7·5 cm Pak 40 was unquestionably the best pure anti-tank weapon used by either side during the desert war (although it was supplanted later by the 8·8 cm Pak 43). With its low silhouette, it was easily hidden, and its 3·2 kg shell, fired with a muzzle velocity of 933 metres per second, could penetrate 115 mm of armour plate at 500 yards' range (96 mm at 1,000 yards). It was also a very accurate weapon and no Allied tank was safe against it. The famous '88' (Flak 18 and Flak 36) was comparable in performance (110 mm at 500 yards' range, 95 mm at 1,400) but its high silhouette made it more difficult to conceal. The captured Russian 76·2 mm guns which, rebored to take German 7·5 cm calibre ammunition, were used in some numbers, were comparable to the Pak 40 in performance at up to around 1,000 yards' range, but their armour-piercing capability tailed off rapidly after that.

German armoured cars used in the desert included the light SdKfz 222 four-wheeled reconnaissance vehicle, which was armed with a 20 mm KwK 30 or 38 L55 gun (as in the PzKpfw II), carried a crew of three and could achieve 80 km/h; the eight-wheeled SdKfz 231 which was also armed with a 20 mm KwK 30/38, carried a crew of four and could manage 85 km/h; and variants on the same chassis such as the SdKfz 221 light recce vehicle, the 232 with frame radio aerial, 233 with short-barrelled 7·5 cm gun and 263 with fixed superstructure and extra radio equipment for staff and HQ usage.

The Panzer units which participated in the desert campaign were as follows (see also appendices): **5th Light Division**, the first German unit sent to Africa, whose tanks disembarked at Tripoli on February 20 1941. Its units were predominantly drawn from the 3rd Panzer Division. In October 1941 it was redesignated 21st Panzer Division with 5th Panzer Regiment as its armoured nucleus. **15th Panzer Division** was created from the 33rd Infantry Regiment in November 1940 and shipped to Africa during April–June 1941, where it was hastily thrown into the front line at Tobruk. The division's armoured core was the 8th Panzer Regiment. **10th Panzer Division** was a latecomer to the desert war, being shipped to Tunisia in late November 1942; its armoured core was the 7th Panzer Regiment (one battalion only). **501st Independent Heavy Tank Battalion**, with Tigers, also arrived late and only saw action in Tunisia. Other German formations in the desert included small quantities of AFVs – self-propelled guns, armoured cars and armoured half-tracks – but cannot properly be described as Panzer units.

The first German armoured units to arrive in Africa were outfitted in the standard European theatre black Panzer suit, consisting of short double-breasted jacket with wide lapels and black trousers tucked into ankle boots, but this must have been most uncomfortable under the desert sun and a change was made to tropical kit at the earliest possible moment. This consisted of lightweight full-length jacket with two breast and two hip pockets, and lightweight trousers or shorts, with long or short lace-up desert boots, sidecap, peaked field cap or steel helmet. The precise colour of the tropical tunic varied considerably from a distinctively green shade through light brown and tan to pale bleached linen. The tropical version of the national eagle in blue-grey embroidery (silver for officers) on a tan background was worn on the right breast, just above the pocket, and medals and awards in the usual positions around the left-hand breast pocket. Collar patches for all ranks comprised two silver-grey bars divided by narrow lines of Panzer pink Waffenfarbe, all on a dark green backing, plus small silver Totenkopf devices pinned to the lower lapels. Shoulder straps were normally in tropical tan colour with appropriate Waffenfarbe and rank distinctions, but black straps removed from the European uniforms could sometimes be seen.

The 'Afrika Korps' cuff title, 3·3 cm wide with silver block lettering on a green background, could be worn by all ranks from the date of authorisation in July 1941. The 'Afrika' cuff title in khaki with silver lettering and two palm tree devices was not instituted until January 1943. Lightweight canvas belts and equipment straps were supposed to have been worn with the tropical uniform, but many personnel retained their European leather gear.

Headgear was normally the tropical sidecap in tan material with tropical eagle, Waffenfarbe soutache and red/white/black cockade (with or without officers' silver piping), but the black Panzer Feldmütze could also be commonly seen. Both of these were worn by all Panzer ranks in preference to the peaked tropical field cap, which was less convenient inside the confines of a tank. Steel helmets, over-painted a sandy colour, with or without army eagle and red/white/black shield decals, were sometimes worn. The tropical topee does not appear to have been popular with tank crews.

Dress in the desert was never very formal, and shirtsleeve order was probably the usual garb. The light tropical shirt had two breast pockets and buttons down half its length. Shoulder straps in tan or black with pink Waffenfarbe were occasionally worn, but no other insignia. Shorts were popular and often rolled up to expose as much of the legs to the air as possible; the long desert boots were supposed to have been worn with shorts at all times but rarely were, since the short ankle type proved more comfortable. Canvas gaiters were sometimes worn, as were goggles and silk scarves, as some protection against the all-pervasive sand, dust and grit. Needless to say, sunglasses were also popular.

ABOUT THE PHOTOGRAPHS

The photographs in this book have been selected with care from the Bundesarchiv, Koblenz (the approximate German equivalent of the US National Archives or the British Public Records Office). Particular attention has been devoted to choosing photographs which will be fresh to the majority of readers, although it is inevitable that one or two may be familiar. Other than this, the author's prime concern has been to choose good-quality photographs which illustrate the type of detail that enthusiasts and modellers require. In certain instances quality has, to a degree, been sacrificed in order to include a particularly interesting photograph. For the most part, however, the quality speaks for itself.

The Bundesarchiv files hold some one million black and white negatives of Wehrmacht and Luftwaffe subjects, including 150,000 on the Kriegsmarine, some 20,000 glass negatives from the inter-war period and several hundred colour photographs. Sheer numbers is one of the problems which makes the compilation of a book such as this difficult. Other difficulties include the fact that, in the vast majority of cases, the negatives have not been printed so the researcher is forced to look through box after box of 35 mm contact strips – some 250 boxes containing an average of over 5,000 pictures each, plus folders containing a further 115,000 contact prints of the Waffen-SS; moreover, cataloguing and indexing the negatives is neither an easy nor a short task, with the result that, at the present time, Luftwaffe and Wehrmacht subjects as well as entirely separate theatres of operations are intermingled in the same files.

There is a simple explanation for this confusion. The Bundesarchiv photographs were taken by war correspondents attached to German military units, and the negatives were originally stored in the Reich Propaganda Ministry in Berlin. Towards the close of World War 2, all the photographs – then numbering some $3\frac{1}{2}$ million – were ordered to be destroyed. One man in the Ministry, a Herr Evers, realised that they should be preserved for posterity and, acting entirely unofficially and on his own initiative, commandeered the first available suitable transport – two refrigerated fish trucks – loaded the negatives into them, and set out for safety. Unfortunately, one of the trucks disappeared *en route* and, to this day, nobody knows what happened to it. The remainder were captured by the Americans and shipped to Washington, where they remained for 20 years before the majority were returned to the government of West Germany. A large number, however, still reside in Washington. Thus the Bundesarchiv files are incomplete, with infuriating gaps for any researcher. Specifically, they end in the autumn of 1944, after Arnhem, and thus record none of the drama of the closing months of the war.

The photographs are currently housed in a modern office block in Koblenz, overlooking the River Mosel. The priceless negatives are stored in the basement, and there are strict security checks on anyone seeking admission to the Bildarchiv (Photo Archive). Regrettably, and the author has been asked to stress this point, the archives are *only open to bona fide authors and publishers, and prints can only be supplied for reproduction in a book or magazine*. They CANNOT be supplied to private collectors or enthusiasts for personal use, so *please* – don't write to the Bundesarchiv or the publishers of this book asking for copy prints, because they cannot be provided. The well-equipped photo laboratory at the Bundesarchiv is only capable of handling some 80 to 100 prints per day because each is printed individually under strictly controlled conditions – another reason for the fine quality of the photographs but also a contributory factor in the above legislation.

The Afrika Korps arrives: unloading a PzKpfw III at Tripoli (425/301/25).

Left Monitoring British radio traffic with a direction finding set (443/1575/16).

An SdKfz 233 eight-wheeled armoured car mounting the short 7·5 cm L/24 gun in an open-topped compartment (446/1908/9).

Inset above A column of PzKpfw IIs. The leading vehicle appears to be an Ausf F and curiously bears the medical serpent and staff symbol on its turret side (782/17/5A).

Inset left The same medical symbol can be seen in a different position on the turret of this PzKpfw IIF, alongside the large letters 'RA'. Note dummy gun (782/15/5).

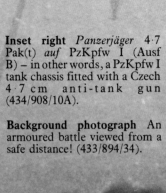

Inset right *Panzerjäger* 4·7 Pak(t) *auf* PzKpfw I (Ausf B) – in other words, a PzKpfw I tank chassis fitted with a Czech 4·7 cm anti-tank gun (434/908/10A).

Background photograph An armoured battle viewed from a safe distance! (433/894/34).

Right Looking at the wheels, this appears to be an early PzKpfw IIB (786/350/2).

Left Pak 37 being serviced. Sand and dust made maintenance a nightmare (783/140/20).

Below left Rare picture of a Saurer *Beobachtungspanzer* RK7 (SdKfz 254) having a puncture repaired. This strange vehicle had a system for raising and lowering the wheels so that it could run on tyres or tracks depending on the going, but it was an overly complicated machine and very prone to breakdowns, especially in the desert. It was normally used as an artillery observation vehicle with motorised units (435/1015/10).

Below Good shot of an 8·8 cm Flak 18 or 36 undergoing cleaning and maintenance (444/1682/30A).

A PzKpfw IIF or G with SdKfz 223 (*Funk*) armoured radio car (433/892/18).

20 mm Flak 38 mounted on the back of a six-wheeled truck (441/1389/5).

A 10·5 cm leFH (*leichte Feldhaubitze*) 18 at the moment of firing (782/23/16A).

Captured Daimler scout car with prominent aerial recognition flag (443/1575/33).

Above PzKpfw IIIE with 5 cm
L/42 gun and, in the back-
ground, an SdKfz 6 towing a
Pak 37 (782/16/29A).

Above left Temporary halt for
men and vehicles of a signals
unit. On the left is an SdKfz 17
(*Funk*) and on the right an
SdKfz 263 armoured car
(438/1186/23).

Left Early PzKpfw IVD with
7·5 cm KwK L/24 gun
(784/207/20).

Right SdKfz 263 with a
cheerful-looking Italian *Bersaglieri* despatch rider in the foreground (782/13/28A).

OVERLEAF
Background photograph German warning notice indicating a
minefield – a common sight in
the desert (786/309/12).

Left inset Heavily laden
PzKpfw IIIE (783/109/10).

Right inset Generals Rommel
and Crüwell in a staff car with
escort (439/1252/36).

Bottom inset Demonstration of
a German electronic mine detec-
tor (786/303/38A).

Above A hybrid PzKpfw III of the 15th Panzer Division, whose red identifying symbol can just be seen alongside the Afrika Korps palm tree emblem. Basically it appears to be an Ausf E with 3·7 cm gun, but it has been up-armoured and fitted with a ball-mounted machine-gun (the latter being a production modification only introduced on the Ausf J). In the background is an SdKfz 263 armoured radio car (438/1193/25).

Above left Another early PzKpfw IIIE with 3·7 cm gun and internal mantlet. This vehicle belongs to the II Battalion HQ of a Panzer regiment, but no divisional insignia are apparent (438/1276/1).

Left A British M3 Grant medium tank disabled by an '88' (443/1574/38).

Right Captured British Vickers Medium Mark II*, an obsolescent design which nevertheless saw some action in North Africa during the early stages of the campaign (786/328/30).

Left SdKfz 263 *Panzerfunkwagen* (424/270/25).

Right SdKfz 261 light armoured radio car (compare with the SdKfz 223 illustrated earlier) (784/202/28).

Below right Lunch for the crew of a PzKpfw III (782/44/6A).

Below Luftwaffe anti-tank personnel pose in front of a knocked-out British Matilda, actually T7208 'GANGSTER'. The young NCO on the right wears the Knight's Cross and Iron Crosses both 1st and 2nd Class (434/945/5).

Right One of the ubiquitous SdKfz 7 half-tracks with an 8·8 cm Flak gun on tow (439/1276/5).

Left A PzKpfw IIF command tank of 15th Panzer Division (783/110/12).

Below left SdKfz 11 light half-track towing a Pak 37 anti-tank gun (782/16/34A).

Right The versatile little NSU *Kettenrad* tracked motorcycle was ideally suited to desert conditions, although only a few found their way to North Africa (443/1575/19).

Below Pzkpfw IVD with 7·5 cm KwK L/24 (782/23/20A).

Panzers roll! Early PzKpfw IIIs and miscellaneous 'soft-skin' vehicles (782/16/39A).

Good shot of a PzKpfw II Ausf F, G or J (439/1274/9).

SdKfz 11 light half-track towing a 5 cm Pak 38 anti-tank gun (782/16/38A).

Good close-up of a *Panzerjäger* 4·7 cm Pak(t) *auf* PzKpfw I Ausf B (434/908/11A).

Left Rear view of a PzKpfw III, an early model to judge by its wheels (786/318/26).

Right A variety of vehicles from an HQ company. From left to right they are: SdKfz 251 armoured half-track, SdKfz 263 (*Funk*) heavy armoured radio car and a PzKpfw III (438/1193/29).

Below right PzKpfw IIIG with 5 cm KwK L/42 gun (439/1279/3A).

Below Demonstration of a 20 mm *Flakvierling* 38 being used against a ground target. This four-barrelled light anti-aircraft gun was one of the most effective weapons the Germans possessed against low-flying ground attack aircraft (442/1457/36).

Three excellent views of an 8·8 cm Flak gun with several 'kills' to its credit, including a ship! (443/1574/23, 24 and 26).

SdKfz 231 armoured car with 20 mm gun (782/19/1A).

SdKfz 231 armoured car (782/20/26A).

SdKfz 250/3 *Funkwagen* in bivouac (435/1013/37).

Another PzKpfw IIIG with 5 cm KwK L/42 gun (783/109/11).

This page Three views of General Crüwell's captured British Dorchester armoured command vehicle nicknamed 'Moritz'. The number plate is rather a mystery – on the front of the vehicle it is WH819834 but on the rear WH81938. Note command pennant on mudguards (438/1252/18, 439/1254/13 and 18).

Right Captured English tank crewman (centre) with his hosts. The vehicles are a PzKpfw II and an SdKfz 251 (785/277/17).

Below right Very rare shot indeed of a Sachsenberg L-W-S tracked amphibian. This vehicle, which weighed 13 tons and could carry up to 20 men, was driven by a 300 bhp Maybach 12-cylinder engine and had two propellers and rudders in its stern. It was used as a tractor on land and as a tug in sheltered water (443/1551/3).

Above PzKpfw III, possibly an Ausf J, with frame radio aerial at rear, and Rommel's SdKfz 250/3 half-track 'Greif' ('Griffon': the German word is pronounced 'Grife' not 'Grief', as one normally hears!) (784/246/22).

Above left On parade. The vehicles are SdKfz 222 light armoured cars (786/347/12).

Left SdKfz 232 (*Funk*) armoured car with frame radio aerial and 20 mm gun in revolving turret (434/908/23A).

Right Oberst Baade, commander of the 115th Panzer-Grenadier Regiment, in a PzKpfw IIIE or F (784/222/20A).

PzKpfw IVD (443/1575/9).

5 cm Pak 38 being towed behind a half-track. Note 14 'kill' markings on barrel (784/243/6A).

PzKpfw IIF with SdKfz 11 half-track in background (782/16/36A).

PzKpfw III, possibly an Ausf G (786/318/23).

These pages Useful detail views, especially for modellers, of Rommel in his SdKfz 250 half-track 'Greif' (443/1572/37, 784/246/19, 784/249/2A and 785/255/10).

Page 48, background photograph PzKpfw III, probably an Ausf G, at El Agheila in April 1941 (784/207/30).

Page 48, inset PzKpfw IVD at speed (783/147/2).

Page 49, top inset Pak 37 being demonstrated to an Arab sheik (783/138/37).

Page 49, bottom inset Wellladen SdKfz 232 (Funk) (783/125/10).

Above Good close-up of a PzKpfw IIF (782/6/14).

Right Something of a curiosity, this. I'm uncertain what the vehicle is, but that apart, what is the SS 'Das Reich' marking doing in between the Afrika Korps palm and 15th Panzer Division emblems, and what colour is it? If anyone has any ideas I'd love to hear from them (439/1254/9).

Facing page German artillery-men with an Italian *Cannone da 75/46CA modello 34* anti-air-craft gun (432/777/19 and 435/1016/15).

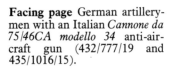

53

Above PzKpfw IIIG (786/313/39).

Left Good shot for uniform enthusiasts of a group of Afrika Korps officers. Note goggles worn by all three men (782/23/9A).

Right SdKfz 231 armoured car with 20 mm gun (782/19/3A).

Below PzKpfw III on the move (434/912/24).

PzKpfw IVD (782/6/16).

An SdKfz 251 crossing the railway line which runs along the north African coastline (786/308/2).

The Fieseler Storch was widely used as an ambulance as well as a reconnaissance machine (443/1563/13).

SdKfz 251/3 *Funkwagen* (radio car) (429/640/9A).

Above An Afrika Korps Ober-leutnant sketching inside a Bedouin tent (784/224/5).

Above left PzKpfw IIIH with spaced armour (784/243/2).

Left A break for the crew of this PzKpfw IIIJ. Note the turret markings identifying it as an HQ vehicle, 1st Battalion, Panzer Regiment 8, 15th Panzer Division (438/1187/1).

Right Column of PzKpfw IIIGs or Hs with short-barrelled 5 cm guns (783/124/12).

Left A vehicle which I did not realise saw service in North Africa until I came across this picture is the Skoda armoured rail trolley, a Czech armoured car designed to run on rails. Here it has derailed itself and is being manhandled back into position by its crew (786/336/34).

Facing page Repair work on the wheels and tracks of a PzKpfw II (below) and a PzKpfw IIIJ (above) (439/1277/16 and 443/1551/31).

Below Vehicle parks in the desert tended to look like rubbish tips, but how much would you pay for a walk around one now with a colour film in your camera? This view shows an SdKfz 251 in the foreground with a Phanomen staff car (complete with command pennant) behind it and a variety of soft-skin and armoured vehicles in the background (783/110/13).

Above The endless desert. A PzKpfw III with Kubelwagen behind it and other vehicles in the background (786/318/22).

Above left British prisoners. Note the relaxed manner of the guard and the inevitable suitcases! (782/20/35A).

Left A British prisoner being interviewed by a German *Sonderführer*, or Special Purposes officer. Note Marmon Herrington armoured car in background (784/232/15A).

Right A smiling Rommel during the presentation of the Italian 'Stella Coloniale' in June 1942 (784/212/34).

PzKpfw IVDs on the move (439/1276/9).

Improvised bridge over the anti-tank ditch at Tobruk, after the town's collapse (785/269/21A).

SdKfz 251 armoured half-track at speed (559/1092/9).

Oberst Fritz Bayerlein (centre) in his SdKfz 251 command vehicle (783/111/15A).

Above Staff car of a motorised reconnaissance unit in the desert (782/41/29).

Above right Nice clean shot of a PzKpfw IIIJ (note side escape hatch) with short-barrelled 5 cm KwK L/42 gun (783/119/20A).

Right PzKpfw IIIH *Befehls-panzer*. The turret number is just discernible through the sand as '101', indicating a 1st Battalion command vehicle, while the 21st Panzer Division emblem on the mudguard indicates that it is certainly a Panzer Regiment 5 tank. Note dummy gun (783/119/26A).

Left Rather blurred shot, unfortunately, of a PzKpfw IIIH or J (783/109/12).

Inset left Good portrait of an Africa Korps NCO showing just one of the many types of goggles worn, also the scarf which was so essential for keeping sand and dust out of one's mouth and nose (782/20/28A).

Inset right Not quite the Hollywood image of an oasis, but still . . . German water cans normally carried the white crosses evident here to distinguish them from petrol cans (782/33/16A).

Inset below Zzzz! Hammock slung along the side of a PzKpfw III (782/44/19A).

Background photograph From photographic evidence alone, PzKpfw IIIs armed with the long-barrelled 5 cm KwK L/60 gun (nicknamed 'Mark III Specials' by the British) do not appear to have been very common in the desert: this is the first and only picture of an Ausf J so equipped which I have managed to find (784/223/6).

Above Superb portrait of a PzKpfw IV driver, but even more important as a rare close-up of a PzKpfw IVE (783/117/15).

Above right Barrel change for an '88'. Wear and tear on gun barrels is always high, but never more so than under desert conditions (443/1587/9A).

Right Possibly posed but probably real – the Bundesachiv contains several prints of the same scene from different angles. Quite what happened is open to question: there is no evidence that the accident was caused by a mine, but nor are there any visible bullet holes. Merely shows that soldiering can be dangerous (782/44/9A).

Left An SdKfz 11 half-track towing what appears to be a 10·5 cm gun (782/18/28A).

German officers inspect a Matilda whose camouflage does not seem to have done it much good! (441/1397/23).

8·8 cm anti-aircraft/anti-tank gun being towed by an SdKfz 7 half-track (444/1672/4).

SdKfz 251/8 *Krankenpanzerwagen*, or ambulance half-track (782/18/9A).

PzKpfw IIIH or J (784/238/16).

Above Included because of its atmosphere more than anything else, this photograph shows a convoy of German trucks wending its way across the sands (782/16/5A).

Above left PzKpfw IIIJ with short-barrelled 5 cm KwK L/42 gun again (783/150/28).

Left Line-up of military talent. Flanking Rommel in this shot are von Mellenthin (left) and Nehring. This is a particularly useful photo for uniform enthusiasts and/or figure modellers (784/203/13).

Right Tightening the tracks on a PzKpfw II of a 1st Battalion HQ company, a nice model diorama idea perhaps? (784/201/12A).

Above From the steppes to the desert . . . The Soviet 76·2 mm gun was extensively used by the Germans in all theatres, although it was later superseded by the Pak 40. This is the anti-tank version known to the Wehrmacht as the Pak 36(r) (443/1672/4).

Right Ve hav vays ov making you . . . enjoy spaghetti? (784/210/1A).

Left *Kettenrad* of a motorcycle recce unit – minus front wheel! (784/226/10).

Above PzKpfw IIIH *Befehls-panzer* – note frame radio aerial (unnumbered print).

Above left Semi-dug-in PzKpfw II, apparently of an HQ unit (786/750/5).

Left SdKfz 11 half-track of a towed artillery unit whose tactical identification mark can just be seen on the mudguard despite the blurring (784/243/15).

Right Typical DAK infantryman carrying his greatcoat under one arm (the desert got very cold at night) and a 7·92 mm *Panzerbuchse* 39 anti-tank rifle in the other (783/123/27A).

78

Left Krusader? Captured enemy equipment was widely used by both sides during the North African campaign. This is actually an ex-British Crusader I (443/1582/28).

Facing page The StuG III assault gun was a rare beast in North Africa, at least one complete shipload was known to have been sunk *en route*. These two shots show StuGs, with their crews still in European-theatre uniforms, shortly after unloading in either Tripoli or Tunis, probably the latter (447/1983/4 and 5).

Below Excellent detail shot of a PzKpfw IVF1 (439/1276/12).

A Flak '88' in action in Tunisia, firing HE as artillery support on some distant target. These four photographs illustrate the process from **background photograph** 'aim' through **inset right** 'load' and **inset left** 'fire' to **inset below left** clearing the breech prior to reloading (787/510/31–34).

Kubelwagen belonging to a Panzer unit (see *Totenkopf* lapel badges), probably in Tunisia to judge from the scenery (557/1022/12).

Pak 37 emplaced somewhere in the Tunisian highlands (783/138/19).

7·5 cm leIG (*leichte Infanteriegeschütze*) 18 in Tunisia (783/142/11).

Italian M 15/42 in German service in Tunisia (442/1451/39).

Above StuG III and Panzer-Grenadiers, Tunisia, 1942–43. This vehicle mounts the 7·5 cm StuK 40 gun and has the early style mantlet (448/2072/30).

Left PzKpfw IIIJ crossing a bridge in a Tunisian village (49/8A/34A).

Right Apart from the Tiger, a second weapon introduced to the Allies in Tunisia was the *Nebelwerfer* multi-barrelled rocket projector, seen here being readied for action (787/505/9A).

OVERLEAF

Background photograph StuG III with long-barrelled 7·5 cm gun, said to be in Tunisia (448/2057/8).

Left inset PzKpfw IVF2 with long-barrelled 7·5 cm gun, Tunisia, 1943 (193/30/10).

Right inset Another shot of the same vehicle (193/30/8).

Left Good view of an early Tiger I with sPzAbt 501 in Tunisia (788/20/16A).

Right Tiger I in Tunisia (787/510/9A).

Below Comrades in arms. An Italian *Semovente* self-propelled gun (foreground) accompanied by an SdKfz 233 armoured car crewed by Ramcke Brigade paratroopers (550/754/14).

Excellent shot of a Tiger I from sPzAbt 501 in Tunisia (787/510/8A).

PzKpfw IVF2 in Tunisia. Why it carries two sets of numbers I do not know (193/30/17).

Another view of a Tiger I in Tunisia (787/510/11A).

One of the first Tiger Is to arrive in Tunisia with sPzAbt 501 (turret number 14?) (550/772/6).

Inset Although this particular photograph has been published before, it has previously been incorrectly captioned as a Tiger I! The tank is, of course, a PzKpfw IVF2 in Tunisia, but of more interest is the SdKfz 252 in the foreground, a seldom-illustrated vehicle (557/1019/19).

Background photograph Very rare photograph indeed showing a hybrid PzKpfw IIIM/N in Tunisia. The basic hull appears to be the former mark and painted in sand yellow, surmounted by an 'N' turret with 7·5 cm KwK L/24 gun painted in a much darker shade (grey?) (788/18/15A).

DAK Order of Battle 1942

Korps troops
(General Rommel until March 1942; Generalleutnant Crüwell March 9–19; Generaloberst Rommel March 19–September 22; General Stumme September 22–October 24; Generalleutnant Ritter von Thoma October 24–25; and Generalfeldmarschal Rommel October 25–March 23 1943): 1st Battalion, Flak Regiments 18 and 33; Panzerjäger Abteilung 576; Motorised Signals Abteilung 475; Motorised Reconnaissance Company 580; Oasis Battalion zbV 300; Motorised Supply Battalion 572; Motorised Water Battalion 580, and other supporting units.

15th Panzer Division
(Oberst Menny December 1941–May 1942; Generalleutnant von Vaerst May–July; Oberst Crasemann July–August; Generalleutnant von Vaerst August–September; Generalmajor von Randow September–November; Generalleutnant von Vaerst November–December): Panzer Regiment 8; Motorised Infantry Regiment 115; Motorised Artillery Regiment 33; Panzerjäger Abteilung 33; Flak Abteilung 33; Panzer Pioneer Battalion 33; Panzer Signals Abteilung 33; Motorcycle reconnaissance Battalion 15; Supply Column 33, and other supporting units.

21st Panzer Division (formerly 5th Light Division)
(Generalleutnant Böttcher January–August; Generalmajor von Bismarck August–September; Oberst Lungershausen September–December): Panzer Regiment 5; Motorised Infantry Regiment 104; Motorised Artillery Regiment 155; Panzerjäger Abteilung 39; Flak Battalion 609; Machine-Gun Battalion 2; Panzer Pioneer Battalion 200; Motorised Signals Abteilung 200; Panzer Supply Battalion 200, and other supporting units.

90th Light Division
(Oberst Mickl December 1941–April 1942; Generalmajor Veith April–June; Generalmajor Kleemann, Oberst Marcks and Oberst Menny during June; Oberst Marcks June–September; Generalmajor Kleemann and Generalmajor Ramcke during September; Oberst Schulte-Heuthaus September–May 1943): Motorised Infantry Regiments 155 and 200; Motorised Infantry Regiment 'Afrika' 361; Panzer-Grenadier Regiment 'Afrika'; Motorised Artillery Regiment 190; Motorised Artillery Abteilung 580; Panzerjäger Abteilung 190; Flak Battalion 606; Panzer Pioneer Battalion 900; Motorised Signals Abteilung 190, and other supporting units.

Other German units present in North Africa late 1942–1943

164th Light Division (Oberst Lungershausen): Panzer-Grenadier Regiments 125, 382 and 433; Artillery Regiment 220; Motorised Pioneer Battalion 220; Signals Abteilung 220, and other supporting units.

10th Panzer Division (Generalmajor Fischer): one battalion Panzer Regiment 7; one battalion Panzer-Grenadier Regiments 69 and 86; part of Motorised Artillery Regiment 90; Panzerjäger Abteilung 90; Motorcycle Battalion 10, and other supporting units.

334th Infantry Division (Generalmajor Weber): Grenadier Regiments 754, 755 and 756; Motorised Artillery Regiment 334; Reconnaissance Abteilung 334, and other supporting units.

Division von Manteuffel (Generalmajor Manteuffel): mixed Fallschirmjäger and other units, including Italian Bersaglieri.

Fallschirmjäger Brigade Ramcke (Generalmajor Ramcke): Fallschirmjäger Battalions Kroh, von der Heydte and Hübner; Fallschirmjäger Lehrbattalion Burkhardt; a Fallschirm Artillery Abteilung and a Fallschirm Panzerjäger Company.

Luftwaffe Field Division 'Hermann Göring' (Generalmajor Schmid): 2nd Battalion, Jäger Regiment 'HG'; 2nd Battalion, Panzer Regiment 7; 1st Battalion, Panzer-Grenadier Regiment 69; Gebirgsjäger Regiment 756; Afrika Battalion 33; 1st Battalion, Panzer Artillery Regiment 90 and 2nd Battalion, Artillery Regiment 190, plus elements of other units and supporting services.

Flak Divisions 19 and 20 (Generalleutnant Frantz and Generalmajor Neuffer). Plus numerous specialist companies and battalions including the 501st Independent Heavy Tank Battalion.